CAROLINE'S COMETS

A TRUE STORY

EMILY ARNOLD McCULLY

HOLIDAY HOUSE / NEW YORK

— • —

Text in italics is from

MEMOIR AND CORRESPONDENCE OF CAROLINE HERSCHEL,

edited by Mrs. John Herschel.

It was read on February 1, 2016, at

http://digital.library.upenn.edu/women/herschel/memoir/memoir.html

The publisher thanks Dr. Matthew Kadane for his expert review of the illustrations.

— • —

To Ethan

— • —

Copyright © 2017 by Emily Arnold McCully

All Rights Reserved

HOLIDAY HOUSE is registered in the U.S. Patent and Trademark Office.

Printed and Bound in November 2016 at Toppan Leefung, DongGuan City, China.

The artwork was created with pen, ink and watercolor.

www.holidayhouse.com

First Edition

1 3 5 7 9 10 8 6 4 2

Library of Congress Cataloging-in-Publication Data

Names: McCully, Emily Arnold, author, illustrator.

Title: Caroline's comets : a true story / Emily Arnold McCully.

Description: First edition. | New York : Holiday House, [2017] | Audience:
Ages 6–10. | Audience: K to grade 3. | Includes bibliographical references.

Identifiers: LCCN 2016035066 | ISBN 9780823436644 (hardcover)

Subjects: LCSH: Herschel, Caroline Lucretia, 1750-1848—Juvenile literature.
| Herschel, William, 1738-1822—Juvenile literature. | Women
astronomers—Great Britain—Biography—Juvenile literature. |
Astronomers—Great Britain—Biography—Juvenile literature. | Women
scientists—Great Britain—Biography—Juvenile literature. |
Scientists—Great Britain—Biography—Juvenile literature. | Discoveries
in science—Juvenile literature. | Comets—Juvenile literature.

Classification: LCC QB36.H5978 M33 2017 | DDC 520.92 [B] —dc23

LC record available at https://lccn.loc.gov/2016035066

Caroline Herschel's father was the first to show her the stars. Caroline wrote about it in her autobiography.

I remember his taking me, on a clear frosty night, into the street to make me acquainted with several of the most beautiful constellations, after we had been gazing at a comet which was then visible.

Caroline was born in 1750 in Hanover. Though the people in Hanover spoke German, the region was then ruled by the King of England. Caroline's father and brothers were all royal musicians. But her mother thought girls should be taught more practical skills. So Caroline learned to knit.

From that day forward, I was fully employed in providing my brothers with stockings.

She was also the family's scullery maid.

Caroline caught typhus when she was ten, and when she recovered, she got smallpox. The first stunted her growth, and the second scarred her face. Her father worried that no man would marry her. How would she live without a husband to support her?

Of all her siblings, Caroline loved William the most. The Seven Years' War was raging, and William would be called to fight. To avoid it, he left for England to make a living conducting a chorus and giving piano lessons. Caroline longed for him.

In short, there was no one who cared much about me.

By the time Caroline was twenty-two years old, it seemed nothing good would ever happen. Out of the blue, William invited her to England where he had become a successful musician. He would teach Caroline to sing so she could perform with his chorus and earn her own living.

After William paid for a maid to replace Caroline, her family
grudgingly let her go. William came to fetch her. Before she left,
she knitted enough stockings to last her family for two years.

The journey, by coach, ferry and packet boat, took twelve days.

In Bath, Caroline settled into her new life, struggling with the English language and customs. William coached her, and before long, Caroline became a popular soprano and, for the first time, earned her own money. As William also needed a housekeeper, she became that too.

By way of relaxation, we talked of astronomy
and the bright constellations with which I
had made acquaintance during the fine nights
we spent on the Postwagen traveling
through Holland.

William wondered what lay beyond the
Earth's solar system. Were there other solar systems?
How did stars form? How far away were they?
Was there life on planets? On stars? On the moon?

To find the answers, William read about how to build a telescope. He wanted to build a better telescope than any that had ever existed. He couldn't do it unless Caroline helped. Of course she would. Caroline became an assistant inventor.

Every room in their house was a workshop. Even the piano was buried under globes, orreries, tools, maps, books, lenses and a huge machine for grinding glass. Building a telescope made housekeeping difficult, but Caroline was fascinated.

William first tried to make his telescope with a glass lens. But it was impossible to make a lens that would be large enough to obtain clear images of the sky.

So he made his telescope with a mirror instead of a lens. At the time, mirrors were made out of metal. William built a furnace to melt tin and brass for the mirror and then fired the mirror in a mold. The mold had to be made of dried horse manure. Caroline's job was to pound and sift the manure by hand.

It was an endless piece of work and served me for many an hour's exercise.

After the mirror was fired, it had to be polished with pitch to make it concave. William couldn't pause, even for a minute, or the mirror would mist over and be ruined. While William doggedly polished, sometimes for sixteen hours straight, Caroline took care of William's needs.

I was constantly obliged to feed him by putting victuals by bits into his mouth.

She read to him too.

Their first telescope was five feet long, with a six-inch mirror that magnified 6,000 times! William would look through the telescope and call out his observations, and Caroline wrote them down.

They discovered that the great blurry disc of light called the Milky Way was made of millions of stars!

Theirs was the best telescope in the world. They used it as often as possible, no matter what the weather. In the winter, Caroline's ink froze.

On March 13, 1781, William saw something new. It might be a planet. But no new planet had been discovered for thousands of years!

It *was* a planet! Word of the planet Uranus circulated around the world and made William famous. It started a rage for astronomy too.

An excited King George III and his family visited the Herschels and ordered four telescopes from William.

King George appointed William King's Astronomer and paid him an annual salary. His music career ended. That meant Caroline's income from singing ended too. Caroline was glad for William but worried for herself. She had been so proud of the money she earned.

William needed Caroline's help more than ever. He began a "sweep" of the sky, section by section. To do it, he made a twenty-foot telescope. William had to perch high in the air on rickety scaffolding, often in strong winds. Once, as he was climbing down, the whole apparatus collapsed. William was nearly crushed.

Another time, Caroline ran in the snow, slipped and fell.

At each end of the machine or trough was an iron hook, such as butchers use for hanging their joints upon, and having to run in the dark on ground covered a foot deep with melting snow, I fell on one of these hooks, which entered my right leg above the knee. My brother's call, "Make haste," I could only answer by a pitiful cry, "I am hooked!"

Caroline pulled the hook out of her leg herself. She continued to work on their star catalogue while her wound healed.

William made a small telescope for Caroline. He taught her math so she could calculate the positions of stars.

I found I was to be trained for an assistant-astronomer . . . I was "to sweep for comets." Caroline always did whatever her brother asked.

In 1783, Caroline discovered fourteen previously unknown nebulae and star clusters and two new galaxies.

All this time, Caroline also did needlework and sewing, kept William's accounts and cleaned all the equipment.

In 1786, William went to visit astronomers around Europe. Left by herself, Caroline promptly discovered a comet.

Last night, December 21st, at 7ʰ 45ˈ, I discovered a comet.... This morning, between five and six, I saw it again.

It was called "the Lady's Comet," and it made Caroline famous. She was the second Herschel to amaze the world.

In 1788, William announced he would marry. Caroline tried not to show her sadness.

William no longer needed Caroline to be his housekeeper, so William offered to pay her as his assistant. Caroline refused. She wanted a salary from the King, like William's.

King George agreed, and Caroline Herschel became the first professional woman scientist. While working for the King, Caroline discovered seven more comets.

Her celebrity spread even farther and caused a worldwide enthusiasm for comets. Caroline Herschel has been known ever since as the Hunter of Comets.

NOTE

The Astronomer Royal said of the Herschels, William and Caroline, "which was the planet and which was the moon?" They were true collaborators, making astronomy a modern science with their rigorous observations and calculations. They found 2,500 nebulae, as well as all of Caroline's comets and William's planet and much else. The catalogue of the sky that Caroline Herschel created became a standard reference work for succeeding astronomers.

When William died in 1822, Caroline was grief-stricken. With no reason to remain in England, she moved back to Hanover. Her fame followed her. She was admired and consulted by scientists for the rest of her ninety-eight years. Caroline Herschel was made an Honorary Fellow of England's Royal Astronomical Society and awarded its Gold Medal.

Caroline died in 1848 and was buried with a lock of William's hair.

Caroline's outspoken autobiography tells of the trials of her childhood and her love for William and astronomy. It makes her prickly personality vivid for us, centuries later.

BIBLIOGRAPHY

Alic, Margaret, *Hypatia's Heritage*, Beacon, Boston, 1986

Holmes, Richard, *The Age of Wonder*, Random House, NY, 2009

Hoskin, Michael, *Discoverers of the Universe*, Princeton University Press, 2011

Hoskin, Michael, *The Herschel Partnership*, Science History Publications, Cambridge, England, 2003

http://amazingspace.org/resources/explorations/groundup/lesson/scopes/herschel/

http://digital.library.upenn.edu/women/herschel/memoir/memoir.html

http://ecuip.lib.uchicago.edu/multiwavelength-astronomy/optical/history/index.html

herschelmuseum.org.uk/

GLOSSARY

astronomy: the study of space and celestial objects. In modern times, it has been joined by astrophysics, the study of the evolution of the universe and what may lie beyond it.

comet: an icy space object that heats up when passing the sun, making its atmosphere visible

constellation: a grouping of stars that appear near one another when viewed from Earth

galaxy: a system of stars and other matter, bound by gravity, such as the Milky Way

nebulae: clouds of dust and gases in space. In the Herschels' time, galaxies were thought to be nebulae.

orrery: a model of the solar system

packet boat: a small vessel carrying mail, passengers and some freight pitch: a black substance derived from coal tar

planet: an object whose gravity has made it round and that orbits a star

scullery: a workroom off a kitchen for washing dishes and clothes, ironing and similar jobs

solar system: our neighborhood in space; all the planets, stars, etc., that orbit our sun

star cluster: groups of stars, bound by gravity

sweep: to methodically examine the sky, section by section, with a telescope

typhus: a highly infectious bacterial disease that raged in epidemics for centuries. Its cause wasn't discovered until 1916.

victuals: food

TIMELINE

1608 The earliest working telescope appears. Hans Lippershey is given credit for its invention, though others have also claimed to have discovered it.

1609 Galileo (1564–1642) was the first to examine the sky with a telescope. (Before that, people used telescopes to see long distances on Earth.) He could make out a ribbon of light that was the Milky Way and craters on the moon.

1738 William Herschel is born on November 15.

1750 Caroline Herschel is born on March 16.

1772 Caroline goes to England.

1781 William discovers the planet Uranus.

1783 William gives Caroline her own telescope.

1785–1789 Caroline and William build the Great Forty-Foot telescope.

1786 On August 1, Caroline discovers her first of eight comets.

1787 Caroline receives a salary from King George III. She is the first woman to receive a salary for scientific research.

1822 William dies on August 25.

1828 Caroline is the first woman to be awarded the Gold Medal of England's Royal Astronomical Society.

1839 The Great Forty-Foot telescope is dismantled.

1848 Caroline dies on January 9.

1990 The Hubble telescope is deployed in space.

2009–2013 The orbiting Herschel Space Observatory sends infrared images from deep in the universe. It was named for William Herschel to honor his discovery in 1800 of infrared wavelengths invisible to the human eye.

2018 The James Webb telescope will be launched on a rocket. It will have 18 mirrors and be able to send images that will help astronomers to better understand the history (and future) of the universe.